VIEW
FROM
MOUNT
DIABLO

RALPH THOMPSON

VIEW
FROM
MOUNT
DIABLO

PEEPAL TREE

First published in Great Britain in 2003
Peepal Tree Press Ltd
17 King's Avenue
Leeds LS6 1QS

ISBN 1-900715-81-3

For the grandchildren
Nicholas, Sean, Natalie, Catherine, Oskar,
Matthew
Alexandra and Sean Joseph
in the hope that the mist will have lifted
when they come to the view

Priests, examining the entrails of birds,
Found the heart misplaced, and seeds
As black as death, emitting a strange odor.

Louis Simpson

PROLOGUE

The light that I have so long loved turns
its gaze grudgingly from the old, romantic view
of islands, from the stubbled silver sheen of mountains
guarding valleys waking from their sleep, dew

overflowing the green uplifted chalice of a leaf,
dangling at each new morning's edge, testing
the gravity of calyx, bud and beaded stem;
turns from pious villages at night cupping

their candles in steep procession down a mountain path,
a girl's giggle muffled in the forest's throat;
turns, confused, from the embracing absolution of a
forgiving ocean washing colonial guilt

like seaweed from a moon-glazed beach. Now the dream
is draining from the valley shadows, edges hardening
as the light changes to a harsh, uncompromising glare.
This day's sun is turning cynical, taking

its early morning tally in the tarnished air, a complacent
prison warder twisting a thumbprint into Kingston's face –
at high noon a hawk circling a laden
feeding tree, pure scrutiny without a trace

of insight, glint of a grin from the muzzle of a gun
as a black Clint Eastwood mocks the killing field
and runs that macho fable through another version.
This light scars the earth, a gaze held

unblinking to wither myth and drain the sap
from trees. Wordsworth could not survive a squint
at it. Pan the goat god has sworn allegiance
to the devil's party, swapped his simple flute

for an amplifier blasting fifteen hundred watts
but after all the raucous questions, a rumour
lingers, haunting the land, circulating a hiss
of whispers. In the city's bursting funeral parlours

the corpses glow at night, a nimbus of blue
acetylene burning the darkness under the roof,
lighting up the windows – crunch of bone and sinew
as a foot curls slowly into a cloven hoof.

To keep the awful secret, they are buried in their boots
but under the leather the light still glows, even
as coarse, animal hair begins to bristle
around the ankles, to sprout along the shins.

CHAPTER ONE

Next door in guinea grass he trampled down
a bed under a gawky lignum vitae tree,
its crown knotted with perky purple blossoms
like the silk bows in Nellie Simpson's head when she

was dressed for church, and there, lying on his back,
sucking a sweet stalk, dizzy with delight,
he felt the sky tilt as the sun singed
a cloud shaped like his island home, a flight

of ardent butterflies jerking yellow triangles
through his eyes. Not even Nellie would dare
invade this hiding place, too terrified of lizards.
At seventeen, nubile Nellie was seven years

his senior, trainee domestic, hired to bathe him
in a portable tin tub moored daily on the lawn.
In public she used a porous strainer pod
to scrub his arms and back but when they were alone

her black fingers roamed his private parts
exciting them with predatory glee
into a generous lather of carbolic soap.
She squinted through a right eye permanently

cast to starboard in an unnavigable sea
of sideways glances – arrogant or frolicsome
he was never sure. It was confusion, fuss,
that urged him to his exclusive grass asylum,

welcomed inside the boundaries of a vacant lot
where the shape of leaves was sharp and clear against
a candid sky, where he could grasp the heft
and larger sense of argument, dream, forecast

his destined role in some supreme adventure
which might demand a final martyrdom. Crisis
starched these years of his upbringing, Hitler
and Bustamante names that reverberated through his house

built three feet above the ground. The lower
walls were decorated with a random screed of octagons
etched in brown, the verandah three steps up,
polished to a garish red, the garden beds dense

with decaying cannas. When classes at his school
were suddenly dismissed, the boys sent home, he had hopped
a tram and on the lurching ride down South Camp road
the image of sweating, red-faced soldiers, eyes doped

with heat, packing sandbags beside the tram tracks,
flashed like a movie sequence between the holding
posts, froze and hardened into memory –
incredible phenomenon of white men labouring

in public. That night his father paced the verandah
deep in the rhetoric of rum. "Traitor! Traitor!"
he shouted to the cannas, "Taking unfair advantage
of the war... England's back against the wall ... the Governor

should throw Busta's ass in jail." Except
for that sequestered, guinea grass garden of Eden
he called his own, kingdom of make-believe and dreams,
evil seemed to be seeping under the skin

of the world. He would take Holy Orders, become
a priest whose worthy hands would lift the host,
whose lips would preach repentance and salvation – especially
for Nellie Simpson who would surely need it most.

"Adam Cole, Adam Cole," a woman's voice was calling
at once cajoling, urgent and commanding, so he
sneaked back home, resigned to Nellie's patronage,
a sweet breeze still blowing steady from the sea.

CHAPTER TWO

Late afternoons, the shortwave GE radio
with round shoulders and satin fretwork face
crackled with news of war, the *Hood* sunk,
Coventry devastated. The hectic pace

of Kingston slowed, then stalled as German submarines
picketed the peaceful Caribbean sea, sinking
so many tankers the flow of oil and gasolene
gurgled to a trickle – meshing gears, honking

horns, the swish of motorcar tyres silenced,
chassis dismantled, cars converted to coaches
fitted with shafts to be drawn by horses. He lost
his lot to a Victory garden latticed with fences

for chickens and goats, turkeys and ducklings; forked
and manured for pumpkins and peppers, dasheen and corn
but a sweet breeze still blew steady from the sea.
At night, the calico air raid curtains drawn,

the stars blazed brighter and the moon smiled down. He felt
the sparse face and crotch hairs begin to thicken,
his heated imagination nudge the elusive edge
of mysteries, the quest for answers quicken.

His German uncle, married to his mother's sister,
had swapped the Alster for the Rio Cobre a decade
before a shrill, frenetic voice proclaimed
to his people *Deutschland uber alles* and betrayed

their trust. Uncle Johann traded in cutlery
and heavy Bavarian crystal. When he spoke spittle
foamed at the corners of his chiselled mouth, the gutturals
his tongue could not forget exploding little

bubbles on his lips. He was at peace in Portland
with his Jamaican wife but sometimes, before
the bastinado of the barking dogs at dawn, he seemed
to hear a fist pounding on a Berlin door,

a squad goose-stepping down a cobbled cul-de-sac,
a victim's muffled sobbing and, loudest of all,
the silence of citizens whose time had not yet come,
an ancient Jew butting a wailing wall.

.

The regimental major who served the detention order
addressed Johann in stilted, high school German,
allowed him an hour to pack and say good-bye,
saluted his wife and waited for him in the garden.

They took him to a camp within a camp in Kingston,
huts stranded behind barbed wire fences, ordered
to cinch for the duration aliens and rabble-rousers,
unpatriotic labour agitators. He shared

a hut and chores with Bustamante. The labour leader
cooked for the camp and the exiled German merchant
washed up cups and plates he had sold before
the war at bargain prices to a nervous adjutant.

Ironies thrived like weeds inside the camp
and in Adam Cole's confused and questing mind.
How to tell a good Hun from a bad Hun —
that was the day's conundrum chasing round

inside his brain. He rode his Hercules bike
into the camp. The fusilier, bored, indulgent,
allowed him to park beside the knuckled fence,
a crimson sun setting at his back, the cantonment

filling up with khaki shadows. He whistled for Johann
but Busta came instead, striding across
the deserted compound, hair electrified, on end,
cotton shirt unbuttoned to the waist. Through a loose

strand of wire he took the boy's hand
in his, sleeves rolled half-way to the elbows.
His cheeks glowed a creamy, custard-apple pink.
Adam kicked a tyre of his bike, in a low

voice blurted the crucial question. "Do you think
my uncle is a German spy?" Busta gauged
the boy's discomfort. "The Governor is a racist and a rascal.
When I am out of here he will be obliged

to deal with me. We will all be free soon,
this foolish war soon done, swords beaten
into ploughshares. You know what is a ploughshare, boy?
It is…" His words trailed to a sudden,

meditative hum. "I will fetch Johann now," –
a slight bow, the lilting sound of fetch
courtly and old fashioned. He watched his uncle cross
the compound dressed in striped pajamas, each

step deliberate. Was he trying to make some awkward,
stubborn Germanic statement? "I was sleeping,"
he explained and lit a cigarette. Adam asked
diffidently, "What do you think of Busta?" trying

to keep a casual tone. "Oh, I like him,
glad to have him in my hut. And he is smart,
no dummkopfesel, ya," the spittle bubbling
on his lips. "A lot of boasting but a good heart.

And a moneylender, a usurer, did you know? When he
gets out, he will buy a big American car –
a Buick he tells me, paid from union funds,
of course. Oh, I am sure he'll go far."

"And Hitler? How could such a man grab power?"
Johann's eyes squinted into the setting sun.
"We Germans have a fatal knack for choosing leaders
we blindly follow even to our own destruction."

Blindly – the word landed on a branch of Adam's brain
like a homing pigeon returning with a coded message.
He wore glasses, understood the loss of sight –
the slow, imperceptible but final blurring of a page,

a denouement disguised, so skilfully delayed
none could predict the sad ending, an entire
generation of Germans tapping white canes down
Friedrichstrasse, yoked like oxen together,

17

ten abreast. Gingerly Adam traced
a finger over a strand of the fence, the same
barbed wire perhaps that coiled its silver fists
from Belsen to the huts on South Camp road, a grim

foreboding that perhaps history was crafting a script
for degradation, a dictatorship yet to come.
The guard stirred, signalled it was time to go.
Confused, Adam waved good-bye and pedalled home.

CHAPTER THREE

Nathan came scampering barefoot down the road
from Silver Hill to serve as groom and gardener
in Adam's home, the odour of mildew and mist
still on his skin, glad to desert a grandmother

whom he loved all the same since his mother was dead, his father
only a name. His smile was seraphic, his eyes
a biblical bright but his tongue for a promising prophet
was flawed, stammering on words beginning with S –

all other letters navigated with ease. The boy
and the groom soon bonded like brothers, dauphin prince
and companion of honour. In the backyard after supper they climbed
a guango tree, their hallowed hiding place.

There, limb lifted high in the slingshot handle
of a branch, they curled their toes into the skin
of the bark, concelebrating cigarettes and secrets,
negotiating lenient pardon for their mortal sins.

One late afternoon without plan or compass
they ventured on a camping trip, meandering vaguely
north of the city until, disheartened by darkness,
excitement blunted by hunger, they crept surreptitiously

into a vacant porte-cochere and there
fell into a hard sleep. They were gently shaken
awake the following morning by the lady of the house.
She lectured them on the sin of trespass but as token

of forgiveness offered freshly brewed Blue Mountain coffee
and scrambled eggs served on the porch, white prince,
black cavalier, an ageing mulatto widow,
assorted servants in the kitchen – all at peace

with the place, plot and muddled history of themselves,
each sharing a moiety of the boy's unfolding adventure.
That year the *Gleaner* reported only one murder –
a lover shot by a jilted Cuban barber.

By noon they stood on top of a mountain, toes
on the brink of a valley scooping out the blue bowl
of its descent to the sea, in the distance, Mount Fancy
shimmering silver, symmetrical as Fuji, a shawl

of mist draped over her shoulder. Nathan's grandmother
lived in a shack built when she was young
by a man who one day stumbled down the hill
and vanished in a cane field. Its thin walls were flung

clay on wattle mixed with cow's dung
that hardened like cement, smoothed, plumbed and whitewashed
with temper lime. The door and window were hinged
with strips of tyre rubber, the roof thatched.

Nathan hugged her. "This is Mr. s s son. He have
a s s strong desire to s s see where I was born."
Adam's eyes adjusted to the inside dark; on the same
wall a picture of Queen Victoria and a forlorn

Jesus, chest dissected to expose a heart
shot through with arrows of light. The house lizard
cringed in a crooked corner ashamed of poverty
as dense as this, the woman unable to afford

toilet paper for the outside pit latrine,
obliged to head her drinking water up the hill
from a stream two miles away, bucket roofed
with cocoa and banana leaves to stop a spill.

O green god of lizards, from the stale remnants
of a shabby life like this what is left for me
to share? The gecko shivered, slithered closer,
head cocked to overhear their stilted, desultory

conversation – would Nathan learn a trade,
return to finish school? Adam announced
he had won a scholarship to Oxford, would ship out shortly.
Victoria smiled smugly. The prophet winced.

"Will you s s stay there long?" eyes cast down, head bowed.
"Five years perhaps." The lizard resenting sacrifice
without reward gazed at Mount Fancy, understood
why God had made the land his masterpiece

to compensate for the utter desolation of its people.
Divine justice of a special sort! Contrite,
the lizard fled. Fog stuck its tongue
into the socket of the sun, short-circuiting the light.

CHAPTER FOUR

Busta as Prime Minister possessed all the power he wished,
power that bubbled and fizzed like the champagne toasts
he lifted in fluted glasses at the Myrtle Bank hotel
or the Cumberland in London, his base abroad, host

there to the British press, decked out in striped
trousers and morning coat, pressing his claim
for colonial compensation. The Brits offered Up Park camp –
ex gratia gesture forestalling future blame

for occupation. He returned in triumph to the island, greeted
by cheering crowds. But there were those who thought
     self-government
small beer, convinced that partial freedom only whet
a thirst for total sovereignty, an independent

land destined to redeem the Middle Passage;
thereafter a grand alliance of West Indian states
sharing black blood and blighted history, the palm tree
architecture of a dream, hubris skulking at the gate.

For all his flamboyant love of shine and show,
his was a simple vision – to increase his people's
daily bread, to match hope and fulfilment in the intimate
adventures of their hapless lives. The formal

drafting of a country's final constitution was not
his focus. His barrister cousin, Manley, erudite,
would argue for the Opposition; a Jew, his party's nominee –
both Oxford trained in law, one brown, one white.

The vested barrister chain-smoked Gold Flake cigarettes,
the Jew sucking on a meerschaum pipe, flights
of rhetoric going up in smoke, blending, separating;
the hub of their disagreement – a Bill of Rights.

The Jew, under *Seig Heil* reverberations of a war
that haunted his conscience, envisioned smoke still seeping
from glowing Belsen ovens, sniffed the feculence
of slowly burning flesh, heard the weeping

of his suffering people, believed that citizens deserved
protection from the State, safe behind a shield
of human rights, subject only to the living God.
The barrister, a closet atheist, refused to yield

that argument. Final power, he demanded, must rest
in those freely elected by the people, the anointed
few in a parliament sovereign, supreme, infallible.
"A Westminster dictatorship," the worried Jew insisted.

After the deadlocked session, they relaxed at home –
Manley listening to Mahler's 9th, emotions
he endorsed but never could express in words; the Jew
deep in his comic book collection, simple sermons

to counterbalance the quillets and quibbles of the law.
He consulted Busta at his Tucker Avenue address,
gusts of breeze from the Wareika hills
fidgeting with smoke from his pipe, in the background, Gladys,

his beloved, who checked his spelling and warmed his bed.
Busta paced the verandah. "I tell you in confidence,
Mr. Hoover of the FBI send me a message
concerning the Black Power sickness in America, a dose

of which is now infecting us. Young Claudius Henry
spending all his old man's money to stir up revolution
here, training insurrectionists in these same hills
and in Montego Bay. There is information

from my chaps at Special Branch their plot is about
to ripen. But before they strike, they will be charged with treason.
I support Manley on the Constitution." He hugged the Jew.
"You must eat more carrots, friend. They will improve your vision."

CHAPTER FIVE

Tony Blake, a/k/a/ the "Frog",
wild white ruffian from Montego Bay, croaked
about his hairy escapades in World War II.
In Jacksonville I got good and sailor crocked,

missed my ship by a day, was arrested for desertion.
The judge not joking, sentence me to death — grease monkey
on a rusting convoy tanker making for Murmansk,
one of fifteen full of fuel, ready

to ignite if you so much as light a fag.
Eight nervous weeks at sea, Jerry submarines
roiling like sharks for the kill. But God watch over
the naturally wicked, don't want us messing up his clean

headquarters. At dusk we drop anchor in that strange harbour.
But more bad news. No shore leave; after
two dry months at sea, no poo — see.
I bribe a craven Russian roustabout to steer

to a camouflaged, deserted dock, return trip
to the ship arranged for first light. Everywhere on earth
whores are the same, smile and smell the same,
cost the same. But I get my roubles worth.

One problem, though. While I was changing oil,
the Germans bomb the fleet, a hundred pounder
down the stack, my boat and buddies blown
to smithereens, lucky me the only survivor.

The Frog's lower lids hung down like sagging hammocks,
eyes bulging like glass marbles. His wife,
a buxom, skin-bleached browning, never stopped applauding
the moral of his fable – the wages of sin is life!

His business now was commercial cold storage for rent.
Two ancient compressors kept the compartments below
freezing, pipes wrapped in asbestos leaking ammonia,
wheezing gauges writing their diaries in a slow

scrawl across a recording graph. Checked
by customs at the gate, cargo trickled
into the warehouse, no taxes or duties paid
until withdrawal – mutton, cod and pickled

herring. That Christmas eve one compressor
died, the walls wept, red lights blinked,
the produce thawed. On Boxing Day he stood
alone among the dripping crates and counted

his losses. He cracked a case open and found inside
a snapper stuffed with cocaine in a plastic pack,
eyes bulging in astonishment like his. "Don't think
of phoning the police," Nathan whispered at his back,

a Beretta in his gloved hand pressed against
the Frog's cold storage coat. "Nice operation!"
he croaked, hands in the air. "Why don't we talk?"
Nathan relaxed the pressure, lowered the gun.

"S s since we are partners now, you entitled to your s s share."
And what had been marginal, ramshackle and tawdry before,
thrived like bougainvillea blooming to full abundance
in drought, overflowing, enough becoming more.

The Frog bought new compressors, relagged his conscience
and his pipes, bought his wife a white Mercedes
and a San San villa. His views on crime were canvassed
by the Chamber of Commerce and other civic bodies.

Nathan, his senior partner, like a mongoose, kept
a low profile, breeding drug distribution
cells across the island, in Miami, New York,
Atlanta, Toronto, London, demanding from his minions

strict allegiance, eyes and guns blazing
when he was crossed. Because of his stammer he seldom
spoke, retreated often to his Silver Hill land
where, if he lived, he hoped to build a home

with a view of the valley. A tree fern tendril curled
a warning on his cheek. A bird's two-note song
soared then faded to an elegy in the evening fog.
The memory of Adam tasted like mildew on his tongue.

CHAPTER SIX

Stoop-shouldered Adam Cole, M.A. (Oxon),
The Jamaica Daily Tribune's star reporter,
tracker of scandals and corruption in high places,
crunched the keys of his dilapidated typewriter,

index fingered 8 and summoned the copy boy.
The story of his life curled in words over
the rolling horizon of the typewriter's pitted carriage –
a pilgrimage from loneliness and the green shelter

of guinea grass where he evaded Nellie's advances,
from Oxford's mildewed digs and gaseous dinners
into the urgent surge of Amber Lee's
tsunami. It had swirled into the shallow harbour

of his heart swamping it, scouring away his crumbling
Catholic guilt. He discovered that power in compression
was stronger than power squandered and his minute
oriental flower glowed with hoarded passion.

But trust once earned, she offered her tiny body
with explosive verve and wit. "Chinese girls
are not inscrutable or insurmountable as you
might think." She unbuttoned her blouse. The pale pearl

buds of her breasts blossomed to flowers at his touch.
At Llandovery they discovered a deserted, crescent beach
curved between the cantle of two embracing
headland arms and in that swirling mesh

of foam lust drained away, love flooded in.
A lecturer in English, she shared with him a conjugal
love of words, the spice that inflamed their marriage,
and the words made flesh – a daughter they named Chantal.

It had been a perilous, wrenching birth, a desperate
foetal struggle. Amber Lee survived, numb
in body and soul and although another miracle
was possible she sealed forever the reliquary of her womb.

Chantal, their jewel, advanced in wisdom, age
and grace, falling in her turn under the spell
of words. They bubbled early on her lips, talismans
she cherished to ward off evil and foretell

the future. But words she learned were victims too...
words uncapped by Adam's father from a quart of rum,
the slurred "L"s falling forward with each splash;
Amber Lee's father in the back room of the shop with his chums

cupping mahjong tiles, the hee, hing, ho
of village conversations filtering through their nostrils
into a staccato screech that set her teeth
on edge; words debased by politicians, their guile

disguised as wisdom, truth stumbling in a fog
of propaganda. Adam's words, crisply crafted
on the *Tribune's* pages, poised there to excoriate
corruption and deceit, were blunted by outdated

libel laws, a Minister of Security and Justice,
more sanctimonious than the church, piously proclaiming,
"If you have credible legal evidence, turn it over
to the police. Otherwise stop the naming."

A pensive Adam lounged on his verandah, the awning
raised like an eyelid afraid to blink. The lights
below seemed to be torches held up by savages
ready to creep forward if the eyelid lowered. The night

waited nervously to end. All was flat,
before him the lip of the sky and the lip of the sea
zip-locked at the horizon. He felt the mountain at his back,
hunched like a vulture, shifting its mass to be

a witness to whatever happened; a prayer half uttered,
sliced in two by an avenging knife hurled
in the dark; affirmation choked off at the very thought of it;
dread contaminating the end days of the world.

The phone rang and words, words heavy with doom
sunk into Adam's brain – Chantal raped
on the grounds of the Immaculate Conception school, the silver
cross, a present for her fifteenth birthday, ripped

from her neck. Sergeant Alexander replaced the receiver.
He had no child. The horror of rape was in
his head, not his heart. Even before the boy
was caught and charged, he understood the motive – a sin

of ignorance as much as lust; the black penis
contaminated, oozing yellow pus thick
with the sick conviction only sex with a virgin
could cure a dose of clap. Silence was quick

to suck all sense from words – poor, dumb
defenceless words! Down a long sombre corridor
he kept hearing the echo of heavy doors
thud shut, one closed door after another.

Amber would immediately take the child to Canada.
All men were vile. He could join them or stay as he pleased.
God refused all explanations. Thud!
Unidentified, the boy was acquitted and released.

Now when he turned his new computer on,
Chantal's face floated from nowhere to fill
the amnesia of the screen, the presence of her absence haunting
his conscience, reinforcing the final defiance of his will.

As the social fabric of the island shredded, the scourge
of words spurred Adam on. He ventured
where no reporter had dared to go before,
lurking in shadows, turning over rocks. He nurtured

informers like seeds in the garden of his contacts, watered
and fed them well for information, lies exposed
by cross-examination. Wounded politicians raged
but *The Jamaica Daily Tribune's* readership increased.

Gunmen recruited by the Party to do its dirty
work were redundant now in post-election
truce. They demanded employment or severance pay.
Still solvent with guns, they accepted an army invitation

to rendezvous in first light at the Green Bay firing range
for special training and possible reemployment. Bunched
in clusters like moving targets on the range, gullible,
they did not see the shadow of a machine gun crouched

behind a hill, ready to settle accounts,
one bullet from the rotating ammunition loop
for each year of service. Only one escaped the massacre
into Adam's sanctuary, a special *Tribune* scoop.

Or the story of a street named for an orange,
flames writhing in Red Stripe bottles flung
into tenement houses, spewing gasolene, wicks
borrowed from *Home Sweet Home* lamps, orange tongues

preaching the brimstone sermon, "Vote for us
or else..." Snipers hid in the smoke picking off
old mash-mouthed women crawling in the gutters to escape.
Water pressure in the rusty hydrants was not enough

to cope with the inferno. Adam watched the wounded piled
head to toe in handcarts, hurried to hospital,
their rings and radios, shoes and mementoes looted,
the voiceless, uncomplaining dead cremated where they fell.

The *Tribune* editor stormed his office. "There goes
freedom of the press. The administration has put newsprint
on official Government quota. One more of your
hard-hitting, scabrous articles, we close the plant."

CHAPTER SEVEN

Trailing a cloud of marl, whiter even than his skin,
Spencer swung his Land Rover chariot down the rutted
estate road flanked to the horizon with field
after green field of servile sugar cane rooted

for centuries in this rich ancestral soil,
bowing now to their stale-drunk master. Last night's liquor
still brewed in his gut, his lawyer's ominous dicta
spinning in his head, confusing retreat and honour.

"You have a little power because you're rich.
But politicians are richer because they have more power.
I tell you, friend, the crows have now outbred
the swans and rule the roost. Strutting the upper

perch, they dye their feathers, preening like peacocks
in a parliament of fowls and fools. King Crow holds sway
in such a cock-a-doodle of adulation,
so stupefied with the banality of what he has to say,

he's forgotten how to fly." He waved his cigar.
"Time for palaver over. We must put a stop
to this black orgy of retribution before they confiscate
our foreign assets and bank accounts, swap

our land for useless bonds, throw us in jail."
Spencer had sighed, sloshed another brandy.
"Fuck 'em. You worry too damn much! Join us
tomorrow at the beach house for a drunk-up, week-end party."

Villa Spencer was bred by *British Architectural Digest*
out of *American House Beautiful*, back issues of which
together with *Playboy* were scattered through lecherous bedrooms
and stacked on the tops of toilet tanks to enrich

the leisure reading of guests. The villa sparkled from the top
of a knoll overlooking the bay, lawns cascading
down to the beach, pink and green umbrellas,
striped towels, white chaise longues composing

themselves into a Raoul Dufy painting.
Light shards glinted from ackee and breadfruit leaves,
from pimento bark, eucalyptus and royal palms
but under the orchard of twisted almond trees

a brown shade settled, so profound it frightened children.
Spencer's Range Rover was first to arrive, greeted
by Bevin, the butler, kept busy unpacking Benzes
as they pulled in. A mountain boy, he hated

being near the sea, feared it, never learned to swim.
But even after Independence he was proud to wear
the Spencer livery – white shirt, black tie, black shoes,
shiny black pants and, for the proper atmosphere,

white gloves at meals. Back at the estate Great House
during his apprenticeship, he was an eager polisher
of family plate and silver shipped to the island
two hundred years ago, all trace of smear

shined off with chamois dipped in Goddard cleaner.
On Sundays he would stroll among the parked tractors
that hauled the cane carts, awesome even at rest –
his earnest dream, promotion to the pool of drivers.

On this Sunday, Spencer, his wife and guests
hunkered in the tepid water at the lawn's edge,
Bevin with a tray of gin and tonics pacing
the beach, mine host cajoling, "You need a nudge?

Can't you see we thirsty, boy?" Bevin prayed
for a brave heart but God was hard of hearing.
Slowly the water seeped into his shoes, circles
of damp clamping his ankles, trousers sticking

to his shins. They lured him deeper in, laughter
gushing at his knees, the sea chucking his chin.
Then Spencer relented, grabbed the tray and spun him
spluttering back to land, back to a dry skin.

"Sorry you watch spoil, boy," Spencer slurred
at dinner, throwing a wad of dollars at his feet.
A gloved hand cupped the reward as Bevin
bowed, long practiced in the liturgy of retreat.

The next afternoon, Spencer's wife, bare breasted,
scampering from sun deck to her room, bucked him up,
paused to flutter white fingers down his arm.
"We were drunk. A joke. No harm intended," the nap

of her contrition unruffled, her smile benign.
She sauntered off into the setting sun,
the sea's silver slowly tarnishing to red.
The taut, unbroken line of the horizon

was thin as the lip of his machete that trimmed
the hedge outside her window, now the burning
bush that had singed the arm she touched. Time
longer than rope, he thought, the tide turning.

CHAPTER EIGHT

Plain, plump Millicent never married,
had no offspring of her own, founded the *Hope*
infant school instead, where daily on the verandah
of the house inherited from her father she tried to cope

with thirty children, greeting each morning with joy,
the Jamaican sun camouflaging the city's swill,
warming the hovels in an ochre glow. But by noon
in that unrelenting, flat light her will

faltered. She imagined maggots in the body politic
multiplying, could hear their rule of sum. Star-apple
blossoms wilted at the edges, bruised and brown.
She prayed divine intercession for her people

split into warring tribes by scheming politicians
parting the Red Sea, the promised land
littered with stones for bread, baskets to carry
dirty water, vinegar on demand.

Noel Thomas, her much beloved nephew from Linstead,
first year medical student at Mona who boarded
with her in term, tried to explain the blight
but concepts like kick-backs were alien to her offended

Baptist conscience. "There are still good people here,"
she insisted. "God will not be ignored or mocked."
But God demanded of her even greater faith
to cope with Noel's sudden illness – blocked

kidneys beyond dialysis, his only hope
a transplant from some congruent and courageous donor.
Aunt Millicent volunteered at once, grateful
for the chance to prolong young life, determined to ignore

all warnings and objections. The tests confirmed a match,
the medical team conferred, the risk approved.
"Into your hands I commend my spirit, Lord!"
The surgeon signalled he was ready, lifted a gloved

hand, nodded to the nurse and raised the scalpel.
An hour later, at a crucial stage, the power
failed and the stand-by generator, under-specified
by an unscrupulous, unqualified contractor,

fouled a valve, spluttered and refused to start.
Millicent died. Noel survived. Word
of the death confused her school. "Who shot her?" the children
asked, expecting a tale they often heard

repeated by a bored voice on radio and TV.
They cried because their teachers cried.
Noel wept his eulogy in the deserted private ward,
his face reflected in the water of the basin beside

her empty bed, the image shattered by his sobs.
And the October rain fell in little shovels
softening the soil, helping to dig her grave.
Out of the morphine mist, the sad vowels

of her last invocation rang in his ears. "Lord,
send them your son, a Messiah, to redress their sins,
to lead them out of slavery a second time
into the promised land of righteousness."

CHAPTER NINE

Senior Inspector Alexander of the Jamaican Constabulary
endorsed with stern conviction zero tolerance as his creed,
despised the heavy-lidded judges nodding on their benches,
the slick defence attorneys, the entire breed

of bleeding liberals bleating about human rights.
He dealt with savages who used acid to erase
a woman's face; Anancy selling the same
land twice; the shifty-eyed slime (worst of his cases)

who raped a half-Chiney gal coming home from school.
For a cop, his face was misleading, light-skinned, blushing
too easily, a nervous smile agitating his lips
always on the verge of combusting to giggles, beguiling

the anger caged in his chest. When the Prime Minister
ordered his presence, he was again that boy who cringed
before the headmaster, pants down. After the beating
came the consoling embrace, justice avenged

but the discarded switch on the ground still seemed
to entwine him like a snake. Then the memory spool ran out
of tape. He knew he was a sinner who deserved to be punished
as did all the ungodly malefactors who dared to shout

blasphemies in the ears of the world. The PM
flipped the pages of the Inspector's file. "Unmarried, I see.
In the circumstances of this meeting I welcome that fact.
We are facing a crisis of crime and violence. The country

is under siege from gunmen and Dons," he smiled,
"yes, some political I admit. But as an engineer
I conclude that a countervailing force is necessary, an anti-crime
unit under your command. Wipe them out, Alexander!"

The Prime Minister sighed. "You will have my total support.
Is that clear?" The Inspector blushed and flashed a salute
that disguised his involuntary grin. Not every man
was privileged to serve both God and the State, resolute

to rid one corner of the world from the curse of sin.
So in that afternoon's hot, anointing glare
history enlisted the man to change its course.
He swapped tunic for Balaclava and bandolier,

merino for orange Kevlar vest, swagger stick
for M-16. The other members of his team
he sniffed out and sorted by instinct, like-minded fanatics,
hungry for power and glory, committed to a regime

of summary executions, the rule of law suspended.
Victims were lined up and shot at close range, powder burns
like Lenten ashes smudging the holes in their foreheads,
tossed in a Jeep, hands hanging over the stern,

fingers writing in blood the tale of their dying.
The wailing of women rose like smoke from the burning
of tyres blocking the roads, curling into the ears
of Amnesty International in London, Adam detailing

in the *Tribune* each murderous spree. "Alexander the Mad",
he dubbed the Inspector but he was deaf to public opinion.
After each sortie, cleaning his weapon, he turned
his eyes to the ring of mountains that guarded Kingston

and saw them flex their muscles in satisfaction,
their chests expanding with pride. That Sunday he raided
a yard and his zeal was rewarded. A ghetto youth
suspected of dealing in coke was caught in his bed

in bright boxer shorts. Hand-cuffed, down on his knees
in the dirt at the back of the shack, he implored, "In the name
of Jesus, I beg you don't shoot me," face angled up
to the morning sky, a dog barking its claim

as an only witness. The boy's muscles were smooth
under a glaze of sweat. A swimmer, the Inspector
concluded, the flat plane of the chest narrowing
to a girl's waist. His gaze caressed the contours

of the youth's shoulders and arms. In his head, the tape
of the headmaster spooled to a stop but the switch
was still on so over and over it flapped.
His lips dry, a bulge blooming in his crotch,

he stood, legs apart, looking into the upturned face,
the eyes for an instant igniting, implying a shared
secret. He pulled the trigger and giggled, blood
blurring his Balaclava, a covenant of silence declared.

Back home, he fell on his knees as the boy had done
and tears tickled the corners of his mouth as he tasted
the salt of his sins but he prayed in thanksgiving that God
had granted him strength to finish his mission. Exhausted,

he fell into a dreamless sleep without cleaning his gun.
But it happened the dog in fact was not the only
witness. Ghetto eyes and a camera peeked out of a window
recording the drama and Adam reported the story

in the *Trib*. The public demanded a Coroner's inquest.
Like the sun breaking from behind a cloud, conjecture
gave way to the dawning and details of truth and the mood
of the country gradually turned against the Inspector.

The Prime Minister reneged on his promise of support, convened
a committee to review the use of excessive force
by the anti-crime squad. Before the members could meet
to consider the matter, the Senior Inspector, in the course

of his duties, set up a strike but neglected to wear
his Kevlar vest and, keeping his hands at his sides,
stepped from the cover of buildings and trees and the love
of his men into the court where Judgement abides,

into an arching of bullets that twisted and turned him
and silenced forever the pitch of his giggle. His cry
for remission of sins was drowned by the fusillade's fury
as he lay on his back in the clearing smiling up at the sky.

The PM aborted the finessing committee and ordered
an official funeral for the fallen hero instead
but as Adam had warned the Alexander virus infected
the Force and God only knew how fast it would spread.

CHAPTER TEN

Tony "The Frog" Blake, front man for Nathan,
a gentleman now by official citation, hosted
his annual Christmas party on the lawns of "Cold Shoulder", so named
to honour his humble beginnings, about which he boasted

with undisguised delight, three hundred guests
milling under the cut-glass glow of chandeliers strung on
the branches of trees to reflect the flaunting of silver
and gold, pearls overcultured by far, hung on

middle-class bosoms cavalierly exposed. Leapfrogging
between politicians, sycophants, cynics and friends,
the Frog rasped his welcomes, bussing the ladies,
bear-hugging the men, champagne glass in hand.

Dr. Noel Thomas, paediatrician, mingled bored
and bemused among the glitterati, uncertain whether
his single kidney could cope with social stress at this pitch,
shocked by the tit-for-tat of cocktail banter.

A woman laughed and clapped her thigh. Class
was the yeast that caused the social cake to rise.
These new Jamaican women from the middle layer
of the exotic mix were more intuitively at ease

with power than their profiling men, more sensual
than Cleopatra. Comfortably at home in the castle
of his black skin, the tribal spoils of party hacks
and hangers-on stirred neither envy nor racial

pride in the doctor. In his world, the children
he helped survive slept four in a bed, sailed
paper ships in dirty gutter water, rolled
iron hoops down pot-holed lanes, failed

their exams but learned to shoot guns at twelve, by twenty
were dead. When he raised a prayer to his aunt, the teacher,
now in her glory, she refused to grant him even
the consolation of despair. It was her healing fingers

that guided his when he poked a child's distended
belly, pulled down the lids of jaundiced eyes.
It was her smile that calmed the whimpers, her donated
kidney that purged his impurities cleaner than dialysis.

General McPherson, head of the Jamaican army,
perhaps the world's only serving career officer
with an osteoporotic stoop, managed to salute
Dr. Thomas. Bent over like a question mark, he seemed the listener

always in any conversation. His ancestor was a book-keeper
from Scotland who had come to set the record straight
at Worthy Park estate, embraced an ex-slave woman
whose African genes were stronger than his to actuate

the colour of his children's skin. "Such a waste of energy,
this," the General gestured, his speech split
between a Sandhurst accent and his natural lilt.
"Will explode, mark my words. Nature abhors a surfeit."

The military attaché at the U.S. Embassy shook
the General's hand, remarked, "Glad to see you
enjoying some rest and recreation," an Alabama drawl
disguising his CIA credentials. A spew

of medals dripped down his chest frankly proclaiming
Washington's interest in the island. The State Department
valued his dispatches based on information discreetly
gathered, some from the General himself, sent

as an earnest of cooperation, a signal of his own concerns.
"Who is that genuflecting to the Prime Minister?" the diplomat
asked. "One of our professors who yearns to have patois declared
our official language, standard English cut

from the curriculum, expunged from our textbooks.
He insists that when the Prime Minister pays a visit to your
President to beg for money he should speak only
in patois – a new meaning to lending a deaf ear."

Spencer, tall, aristocratic, in from the country
for the fete, dusty and hot from the drive, quenched
his thirst with a brandy, acknowledging the greetings of friends,
embracing his favourites. A Minister who regularly lunched

at the Great House and left with a thick envelope for dessert
shook hands. "I can't believe that boy, the butler,
tried to rape your wife. Thank God you heard her screams
and shot the son of a bitch before he could hurt her.

Damn nonsense holding a coroner's inquest. Your word
against a maid. But not to worry. I'll speak
with the police." Spencer patted his thanks on the Minister's shoulder,
winked and reminded, "Roast pork for lunch next week."

The *Tribune* reporter tugged the doctor's sleeve.
"Blake has collapsed," he whispered. "Come quickly, please."
Noel saw the body sprawled on the verandah,
a blue nimbus around the lips, a pulse

still ticking in the thick neck. The doctor knelt,
opened the mouth, and like a black God inspirited
the breath of life into the inert sack
of crumpled linen. The eyes opened, the outspread

fingers collected into a steeple on his chest. Mistaking
the reporter for a priest, he prayed: "Bless me, Father,
for I have sinned..." The confession burbled out
like vomit, Adam Cole, the reporter, leaning closer

so as not to miss a name, a place, a date.
The dying declaration, exception to the hearsay rule,
spooled to a stop. A curious crowd clustered
at a respectful distance and already the hysteric wail

of a siren was splitting the air. In the ambulance, the doctor,
the *Tribune* reporter and the wife rode with Blake
to the hospital but God, swayed by such a rare,
contrition even the devil could not shake,

decided this was the gangster's finest hour,
his best chance to hear the welcoming blast
of heavenly trumpets and angels singing. A providential
clot churned through his brain. The Frog croaked his last.

CHAPTER ELEVEN

Smoke of remembrance curled into Blaka's eyes, floating him
back to his boyhood; village girls hand-washing
their blouses in the river naked from the waist, breasts
bouncing, squishing water through their fists, laughing

at him, trying to make him break a smile;
on a shelf in the kitchen at home, a demijohn of water
and eggs piled high in a yabba, his mother so
distrustful of the neighbours, each day she pushed a finger

up the fowls to check the egg count before they laid.
But Blaka was the culprit using a pin to prick
a hole, then sucking them clean. She caught him one day,
grabbed a tamarind switch and tore the shirt from his back.

"Mamma I sorry" (whumm). "Boy, sorry
is not enough" (whumm, whumm). If you bad
the Bible say spare the rod and spoil
the child. It not easy to love but as God

is my judge you will thank me for this beating (whumm, whumm).
The sermons and whippings increased, each sin reprimanded
by a new barrage until one morning, her raised
arm froze in the air, her heart exploded.

So, a grown man now, when the baby mother
kept ranting, "Blaka, you is a wutless nayga,"
he brandished his machete to silence the sermons in his head,
chopped a red wedge from her neck and when a

neighbour knocked, he fled his village for a Kingston
inner city ghetto. There a woman organizer
for the Party by the name of "Squint-Eye Nellie" slipped him
a gun, commissioned him as chief political enforcer

of bogus voting and the doling out of tribal
spoils to party faithfuls. After the bloody
intimacy of a sharp machete, the gun
was easy – clean, swift, distant but deadly,

between the pulling of the trigger and the stagger of the other
only a slight warming of the palm, a cordite O
smiling at him from the muzzle of the Glock. He served
Squint-Eye Nellie with distinction, friend and foe,

fear and favour balanced in a jurisprudence the people
understood and the politicians sponsored, the lesson of the gun
in one ear and out the other; Blaka
bent to such enforcement, still his mother's son.

Then one day, like a boy alone in a field
kicking over stones, disconsolate, he found religion –
a buried golden coin he lifted gingerly
into the corroded bezel of his heart. The conviction –

sudden, utter, unshakeable — that he was doomed
numbed his shooting arm, misted his eyes.
It was as if his mother, at the other end of the field,
kept calling his name, cajoling him to confess his sins,

not his mother in the flesh but Adam, her surrogate,
who would take him in and grant him absolution for repented
crimes. The new informer's confession filled
two spiral notebooks: Russian fishermen who traded

AK 47s for ganja; bribes and bullets
by the Colombian cartel clearing safe passage
north for the White Lady; the world flushing
its jails of Jamaican gangsters, a new rage

infecting the fight for turf back home in Kingston;
Nellie nervously bracing her corner against invasion.
"*Have Frightened Politicians Lost Control of Dons?*"
the reporter headlined in the *Trib*, to the Party's consternation,

a worried Prime Minister contemplating new elections.
Adam speculated that Nellie, under pressure, might surrender
to the blandishments of the cartel, become an acolyte
swinging coke instead of incense in her censer.

Blaka warned Adam, "This Nellie woman dangerous."
He nodded agreement, remembering the eager pull
of fingers in the water of the yellow tub, the warning
fidget of a black fist against his balls.

She had swapped sex for power as he had traded
distraught wife and violated child for the holier
companionship of words, words slowly turning
to ashes as the passion and the purpose both grew colder.

Then one unscheduled night during a raucous
assault by rain upon the house, Blaka, the informer
tapped on a window, face to glass, cold lips
dripping with wet warnings of impending danger.

"Flee, Mr. Adam, flee. Them buy a contract
on your life. Fly to Miami in the morning or else
you dead.." Nellie perhaps? "No, not she.
Them say before him die the Frog confess

and you was there, write down the runnings and the names.
Maybe the Frog's people buying silence. Blood
cheaper than drugs." "Thanks for the warning, friend."
Damp stained the carpet where a dripping Blaka had stood.

The following day, the air rinsed of dust
by the rain, the morning broke clean and clear. Leaves shone,
shadows and highlights were sharp at the edges, the mountains
towelled off, turning their flanks to the sun.

By the side of the road at Mount Diablo's crest,
under a plastic tarp, they found his body
stuffed in a handcart, head severed, torso turned
to the mountain, blank eyes staring down the valley.

A crow, the early bird, swooped low over
the cart to read the word *Judas*, warning intaglio,
carved with a switchblade into the transom. On a higher thermal
others circled like black wreaths. But keener than the crows,

a pushing, pointing, laughing crowd converged
on the corpse – men in merinos, women panting out of breath,
toothless grandmothers, gleeful children, all
eager to witness and wallow in the morbidity of death.

CHAPTER TWELVE

At noon the nation's radios cleared their throats
of cornflakes and cooking oil commercials, announced
that murder quotas for that day had been routinely
met, each killing routinely deprecated and denounced

in cliché soundbites by the Honourable Minister of Justice.
News of the circling crows shadowed a chill
over Adam's heart, clogging the circuits of his brain,
the horror of Blaka's death chloroforming his will.

Doors kept banging shut, thud after thud.
He was naked in a long, dark corridor, impressed
to basic Being, that ultimately simple yet
vastly complicated state because it comprised

no parts to deconstruct, more rigorous even
than death itself or the vulgar transfiguration
of the informer high on the devil's mountain top.
So feeble now the voice of Oxford reason!

Like his father's Alzheimers, one by one he purged
the memory of his computer. He deleted the stored files
and disks, sealed his diary and spiral notebooks
in three *Jamaica Tribune* manila envelopes

addressed to his editor, each inscribed in red,
"To Be Opened In Case Of My Death." He locked the office,
drove home in slanting afternoon, amber light,
watching age spots on the back of his hands trace

a map of Florida – such a horizontal landscape
without a mountain or a valley. On a monitor of the earth
it would be flat as the baseline of an exhausted heart.
Why would he fly to such a mediocre death?

At a traffic light, a schoolgirl with almond eyes
glanced at him as she crossed, phantom Chantal,
imagined words of censure forming on her lips.
"I was your special china doll but when I fell

you tossed me from your love, chipped and soiled." She seemed
so real he tried to lower the window, needing
forgiveness but the girl walked on, an impatient taxi
honking on his tail, her white school uniform receding.

Nathan was waiting when he got home, lounging
on the living room sofa, a Beretta between his legs.
"You reach s s sooner than I expected. S S Sorry
about Blaka. Religion kill him! Drugs

dealing more s s simple than faith if you play by the rules.
Is a long time we don't talk about the early
days. Grandma dead, you know." He closed his eyes
and Adam heard a distant door close softly.

The eyes still sparkled but under the skin of the face
the skull was beginning to bulge. He talked about
his life in a whisper. "I keep a low profile.
Is s s swagger cause most men to dead. I doubt

anyone s scorn money more than me – no chains
or Lexus, no ten-room mansion on a Mandeville hill,
no high complexion gals. When you leave for Oxford,
it mash me up bad, leave me low. I feel

you desert me, man." He closed his eyes again.
"When the money was more than I could count, it once
cross my mind to leave it to you in my will
but s since it look you might die before me, no s sense

in that. Perhaps the University, a multi-million
dollar endowment in honour of Tony Blake –
'Frog Auditorium', what you think of that?"
He jammed the gun in his waist, began to poke

in Adam's desk where his rosary was buried in a cup
with keys and paper clips. "S s swear on this cross
you will resign from the *Trib* tomorrow, leave Jamaica,
never reveal information about my business.

Is not so drug man usually deal with danger
but I love you, man, will respect your promise. Don't make me
have to shoot you, man." His eyes blazed.
"Friendship really hard. I offer Squint-Eye Nellie

the s same deal and s-she refuse. Tomorrow
they will find her body floating in the harbour." Adam
knew he was in a place beyond words, in a corner
of a corridor without doors or windows where some

crucial secret had been hiding but could hide no more,
where a man might finally know himself. Under
the raised crucifix he threw his arms around
the prophet's slim neck and in a silence deeper

than the absence of sound or possibilities, it seemed that their
embrace became a dance, a twirling slowly
round the room. Then he was alone, at peace,
retreating footsteps a faint echo barely

audible above the whisper of other voices
he had loved, the guinea grass green and he
on his back in the vacant lot once more among
butterflies, a sweet breeze blowing steady from the sea.

Ralph Thompson was born in America in 1928. His family on his mother's side goes back three generations in Jamaica, a mixture of crypto Jewish (Isaacs) and Irish stock (Fielding). It was staunchly Catholic and claimed to be white. His mother's marriage lasted only three years and she returned to Jamaica and brought up her two children aided and abetted by a household of intellectually brilliant but poor and highly eccentric aunts and uncles.

Ralph Thompson's education was heavily influenced by the Jesuits through high school in Jamaica and University in America. After earning his Doctor of Law degree at Fordham University in New York, he served for two years as an officer in the US Air Force in Japan, after which he returned to Jamaica and started his career as businessman, painter and poet. The father of four children, he lives with his wife in Kingston.

He has given public service under both political administrations in Jamaica and was awarded the C.D. (Commander of Distinction) in the Jamaican National Honours of 1988. He is a regular broadcaster and panelist on Jamaican radio and contributor of articles to Jamaica's press.